IMAGINE DRAGONS
FOR UKULELE

Cover photo: Getty Images / Brian Rasic / Contributor

ISBN 978-1-5400-8439-2

Visit Hal Leonard Online at
www.halleonard.com

Contact us:
Hal Leonard
7777 West Bluemound Road
Milwaukee, WI 53213
Email: info@halleonard.com

In Europe, contact:
Hal Leonard Europe Limited
42 Wigmore Street
Marylebone, London, W1U 2RN
Email: info@halleonardeurope.com

In Australia, contact:
Hal Leonard Australia Pty. Ltd.
4 Lentara Court
Cheltenham, Victoria, 3192 Australia
Email: info@halleonard.com.au

CONTENTS

Bad Liar

Words and Music by Dan Reynolds, Wayne Sermon, Ben McKee,
Daniel Platzman, Jorgen Odegard and Aja Volkman

So, look me in the eyes, tell me what you

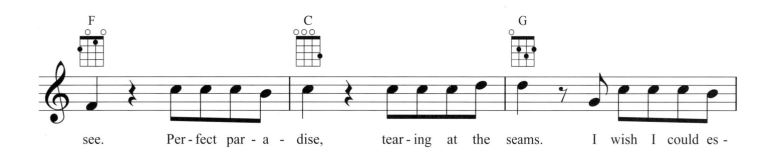

see. Per - fect par - a - dise, tear - ing at the seams. I wish I could es -

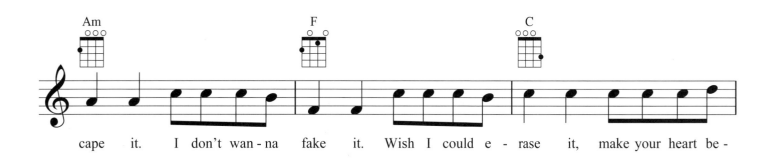

cape it. I don't wan - na fake it. Wish I could e - rase it, make your heart be -

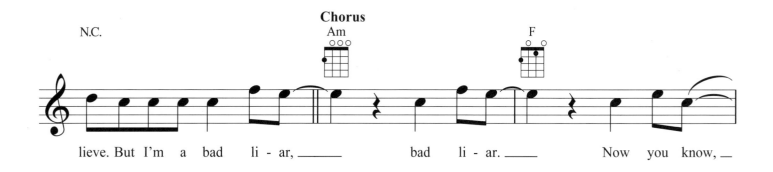

lieve. But I'm a bad li - ar, _____ bad li - ar. _____ Now you know, _

_____ now you know. _ I'm a bad li - ar, _____ bad li - ar. _

Now you know, _____ you're free to go. _____ 2. Did

Verse

all my dreams nev - er mean one thing? _ Does hap - pi - ness lie in a

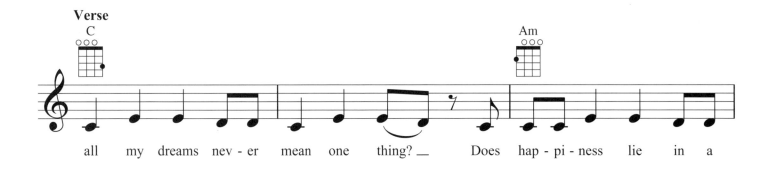

dia - mond ring? _ Oh, _____ I've been ask - ing for, oh, _____ I've been ask - ing for prob -

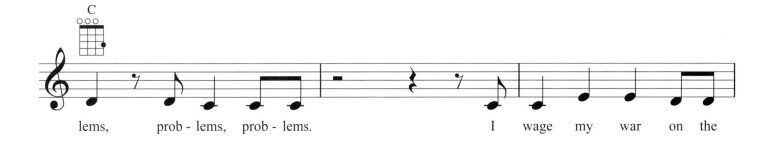

lems, prob - lems, prob - lems. I wage my war on the

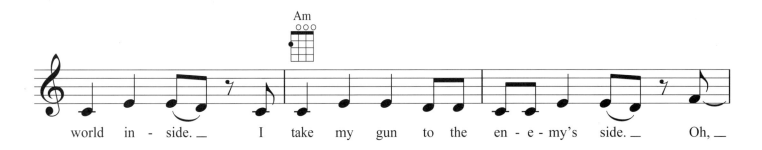

world in - side. _ I take my gun to the en - e - my's side. _ Oh, _

_____ I've been ask-ing for, oh, _____ I've been ask-ing for prob-lems, prob-lems, prob-lems. _____

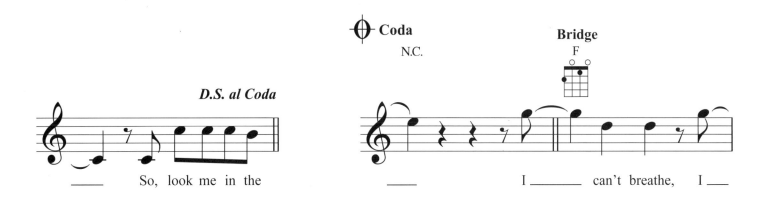

D.S. al Coda

_____ So, look me in the

Coda

N.C.

Bridge

_____ I _____ can't breathe, I _____

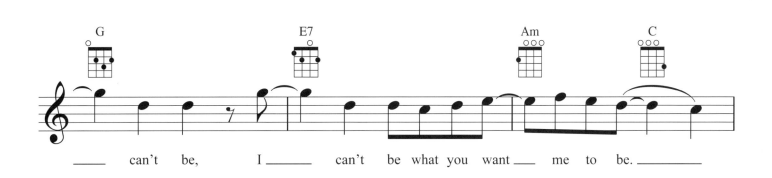

_____ can't be, I _____ can't be what you want _____ me to be. _____

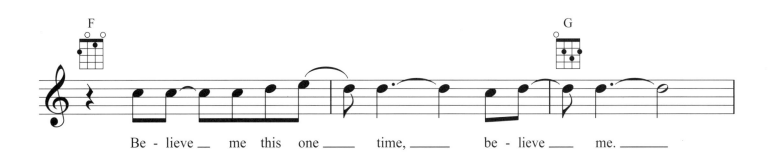

Be - lieve _____ me this one _____ time, _____ be - lieve _____ me. _____

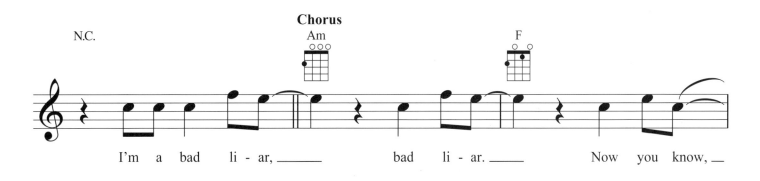

Chorus

N.C.

I'm a bad li - ar, _____ bad li - ar. _____ Now you know, _____

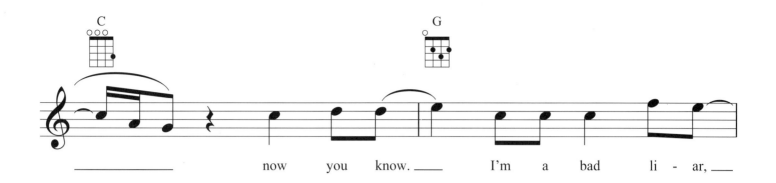

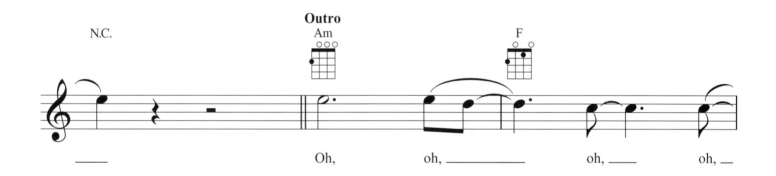

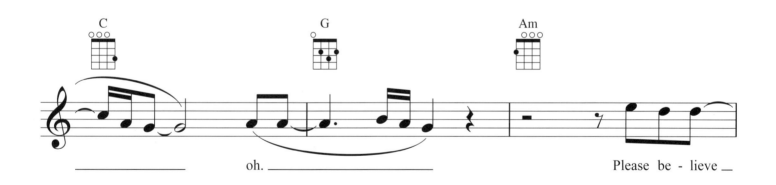

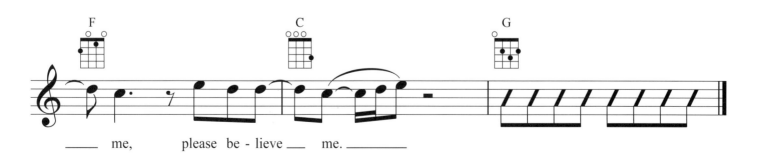

Believer

Words and Music by Dan Reynolds, Wayne Sermon, Ben McKee, Daniel Platzman, Justin Trantor, Mattias Larsson and Robin Fredricksson

sulk - ing ___ to the mass - es, writ - ing my po - ems ___ for the few that looked at me,

took to me, shook to me, feel - ing me sing - ing from heart - ache, __ from the pain, tak - ing my

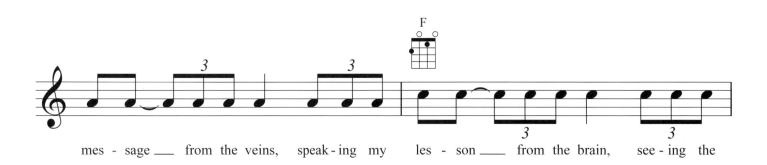

mes - sage ___ from the veins, speak - ing my les - son ___ from the brain, see - ing the

𝄋 Chorus

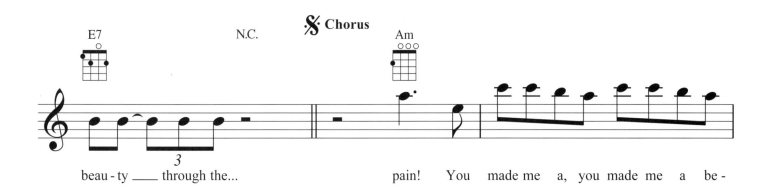

beau - ty ___ through the... pain! You made me a, you made me a be -

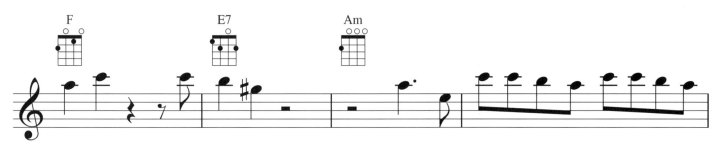

liev - er, be - liev - er. Pain! You break me down, you build me up; be -

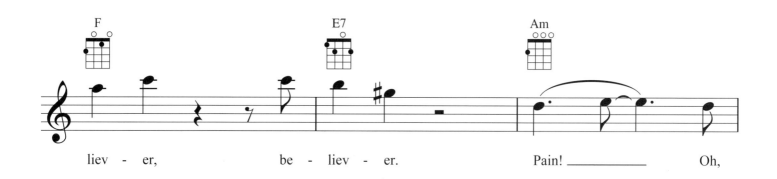

liev - er, be - liev - er. Pain! _____ Oh,

let the bul - lets fly, oh, let them rain. _____ My life, my love, my drive, they came from...

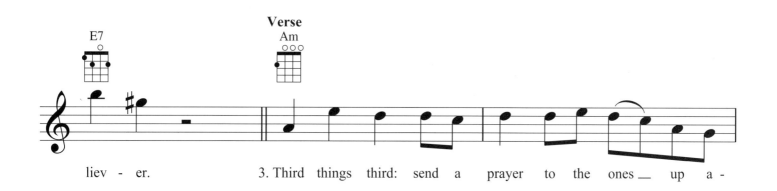

To Coda 1
To Coda 2

pain! You made me a, you made me a be - liev - er, be -

Verse

liev - er. 3. Third things third: send a prayer to the ones __ up a -

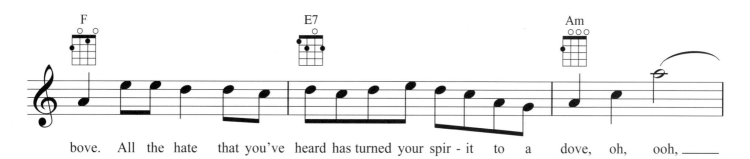

bove. All the hate that you've heard has turned your spir - it to a dove, oh, ooh, ____

your spir-it up a - bove, oh, ooh. _____ I was

Pre-Chorus

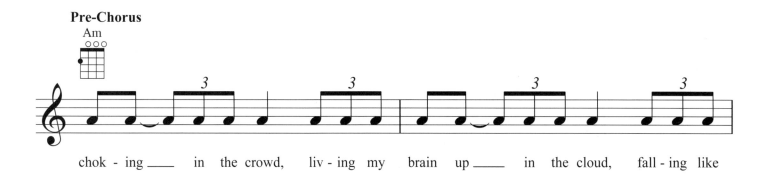

chok - ing ____ in the crowd, liv-ing my brain up ____ in the cloud, fall-ing like

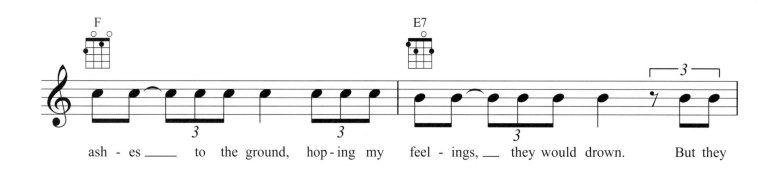

ash - es ____ to the ground, hop-ing my feel - ings, __ they would drown. But they

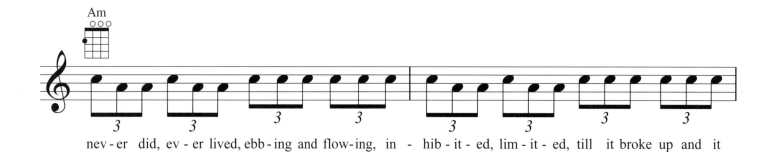

nev - er did, ev - er lived, ebb-ing and flow-ing, in - hib - it - ed, lim - it - ed, till it broke up and it

Coda 1

D.S. al Coda 1

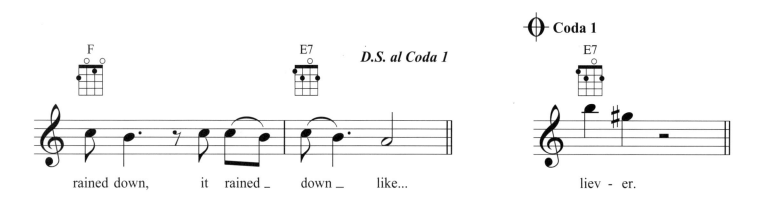

rained down, it rained _ down _ like...   liev - er.

Verse

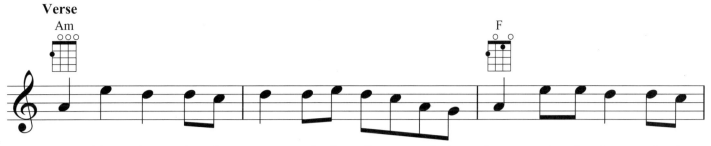

4. Last things last: by the grace of the fi - re and the flames, you're the face of the

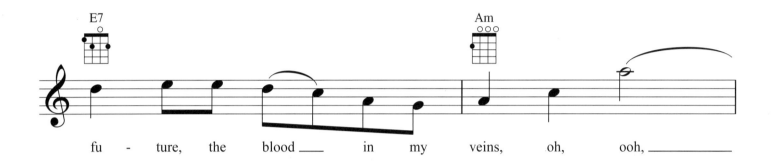

fu - ture, the blood ___ in my veins, oh, ooh, _____

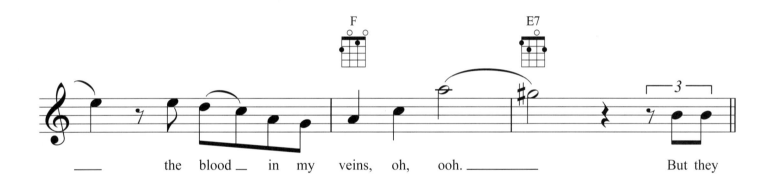

___ the blood _ in my veins, oh, ooh. _____ But they

Pre-Chorus

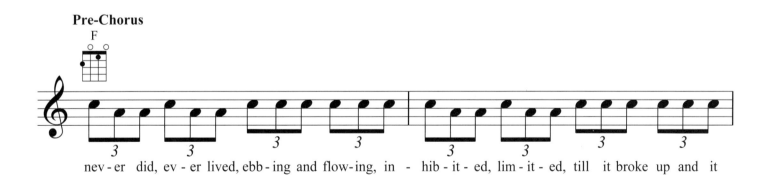

nev - er did, ev - er lived, ebb - ing and flow - ing, in - hib - it - ed, lim - it - ed, till it broke up and it

rained down, it rained _ down _ like... liev - er.

D.S. al Coda 2   **Coda 2**

Bleeding Out

**Words and Music by Daniel Reynolds, Benjamin McKee, Daniel Sermon,
Alexander Grant and Josh Mosser**

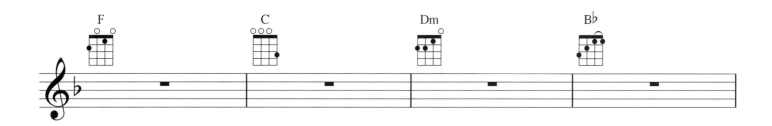

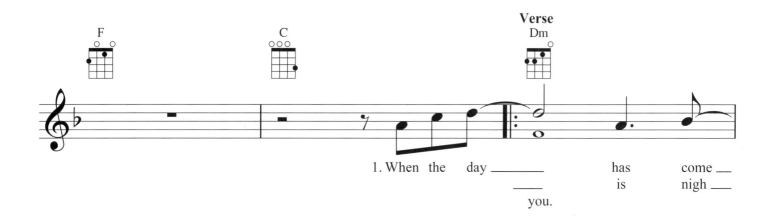

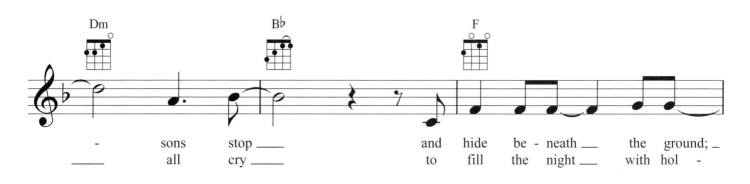

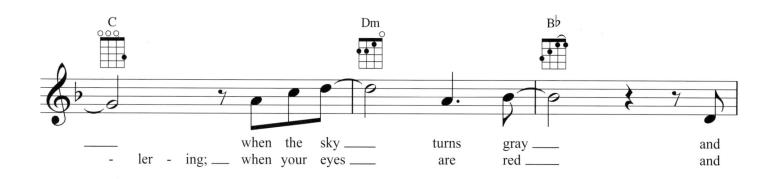

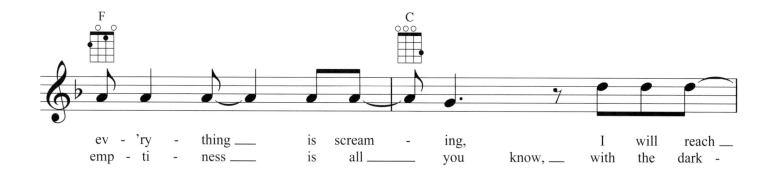

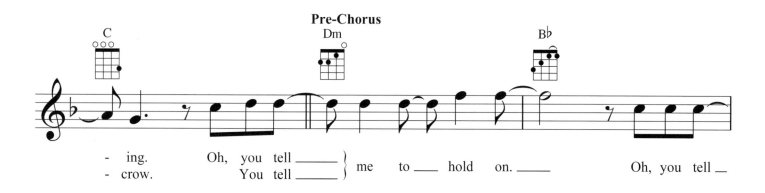

Pre-Chorus

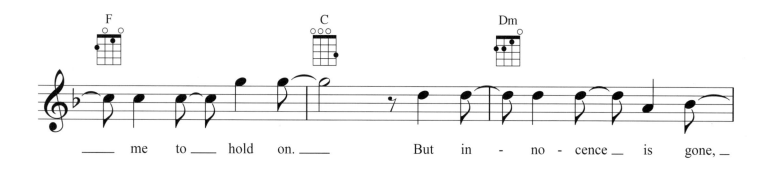

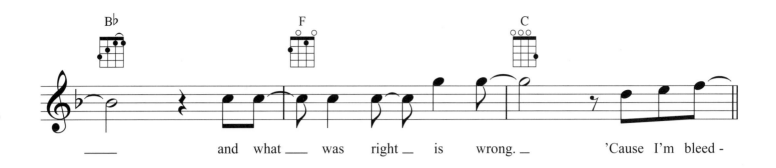

and what ___ was right ___ is wrong. ___ 'Cause I'm bleed -

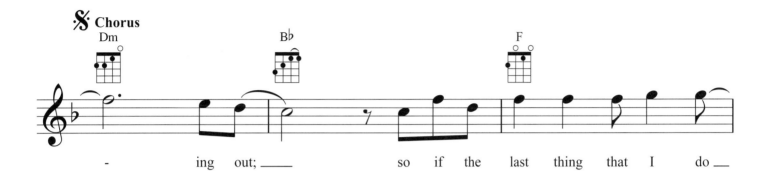

𝄋 Chorus

- ing out; ___ so if the last thing that I do ___

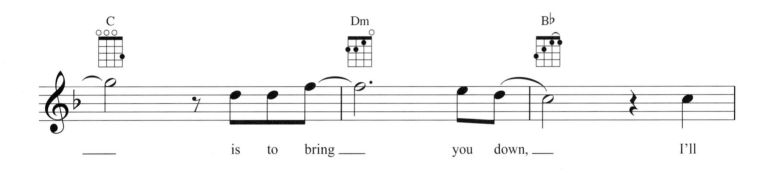

___ is to bring ___ you down, ___ I'll

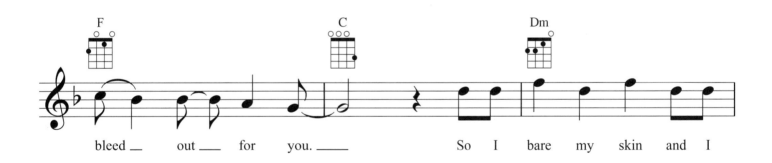

bleed ___ out ___ for you. ___ So I bare my skin and I

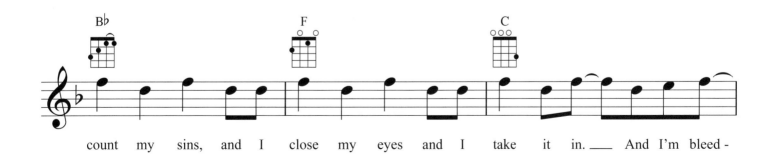

count my sins, and I close my eyes and I take it in. ___ And I'm bleed -

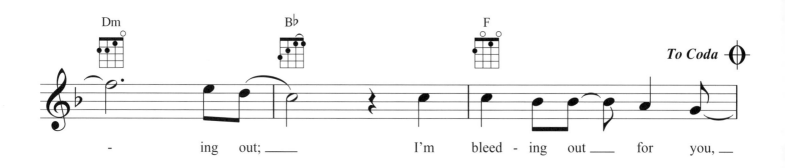

- ing out; _____ I'm bleed - ing out _____ for you, _____

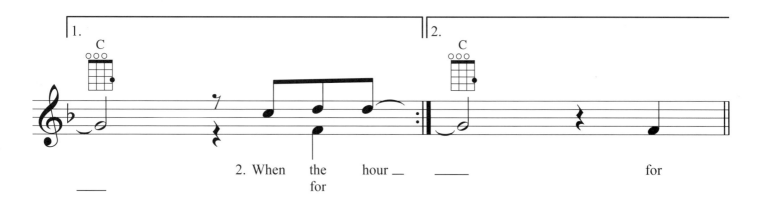

1. _____

2. When the hour _____ _____ for
for

Interlude

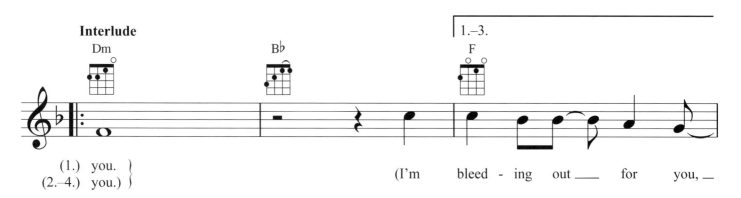

(1.) you.
(2.–4.) you.)

(I'm bleed - ing out _____ for you, _____

4.

_____ for bleed - ing out _____ for you.) _____ 'Cause I'm bleed -

Coda

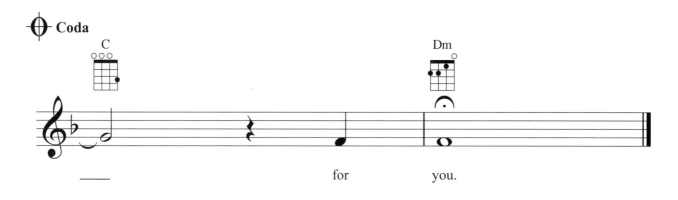

_____ for you.

Born to Be Yours

Words and Music by Kyrre Gørvell-Dahll, Dan Reynolds, Wayne Sermon,
Benjamin McKee and Daniel Platzman

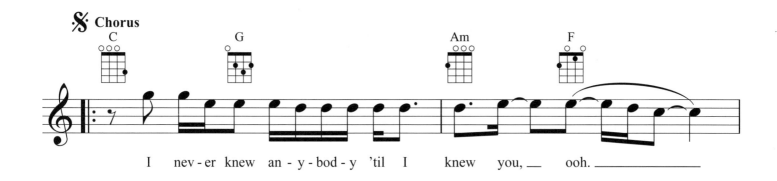

Chorus

I nev-er knew an-y-bod-y 'til I knew you, — ooh. _____

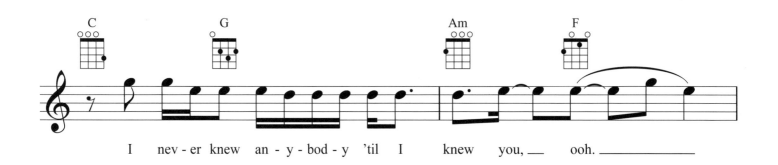

I nev-er knew an-y-bod-y 'til I knew you, — ooh. _____

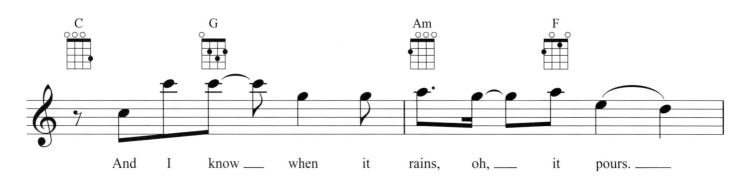

And I know — when it rains, oh, — it pours. _____

To Coda 1., 3.

And I know — I was born to — be yours. _____

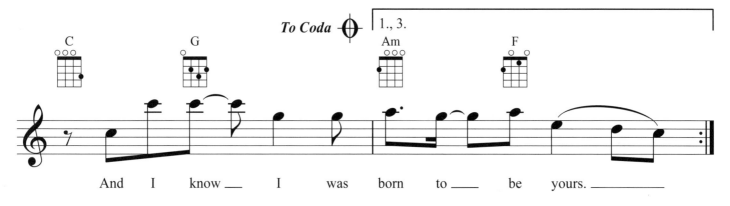

2. *Interlude*

born to — be yours. _____

(Vocal 1st time only)

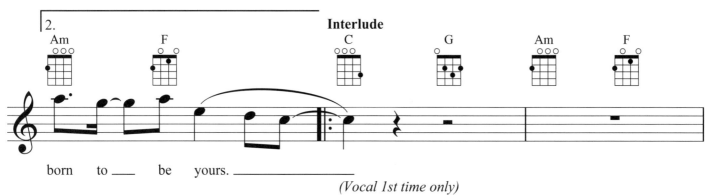

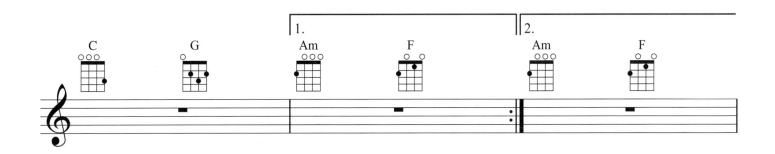

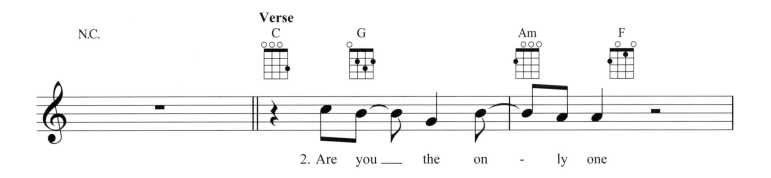

2. Are you ___ the on - ly one

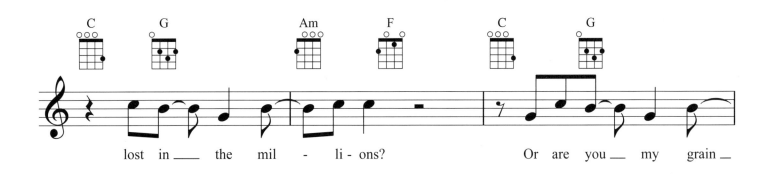

lost in ___ the mil - li - ons? Or are you ___ my grain ___

D.S. al Coda
(with repeat)

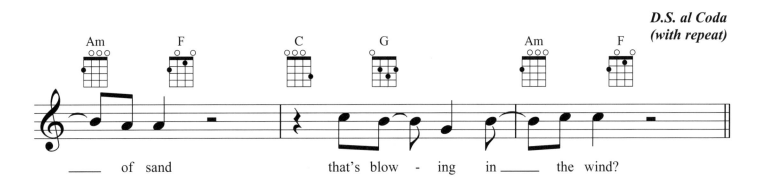

___ of sand that's blow - ing in ___ the wind?

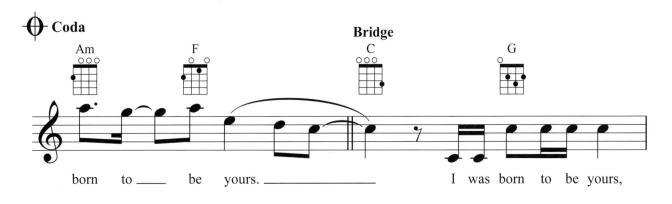

born to ___ be yours. ___ I was born to be yours,

I was born, born, born, born. I was born to be yours,

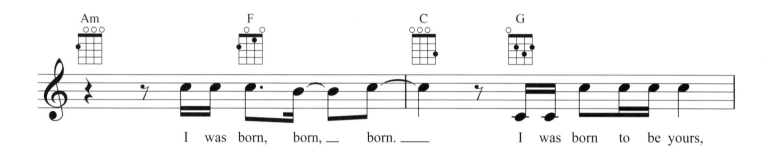

I was born, born, born. I was born to be yours,

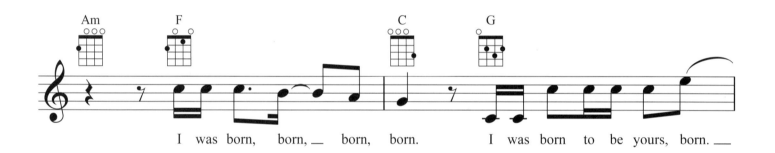

I was born, born, born, born. I was born to be yours, born.

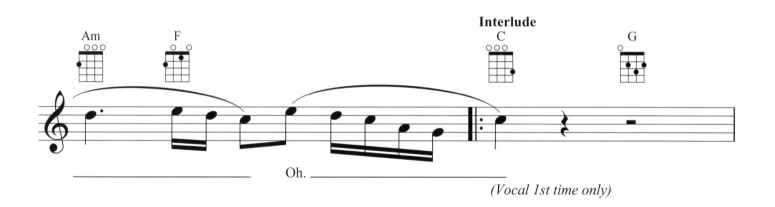

Interlude

Oh.

(Vocal 1st time only)

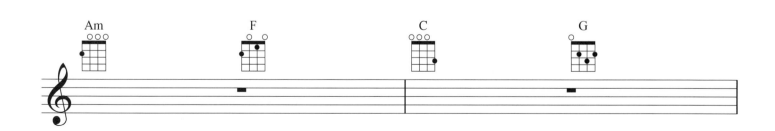

22

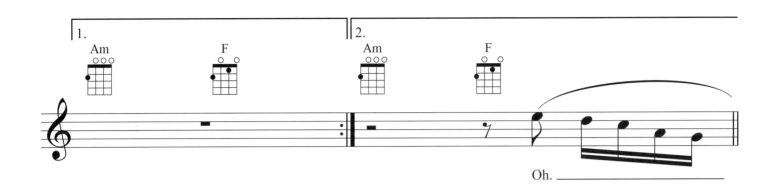

Oh. _____

Outro-Bridge

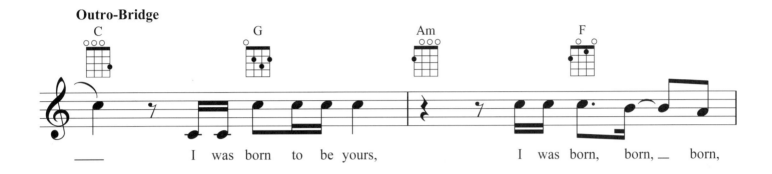

_____ I was born to be yours, I was born, born, __ born,

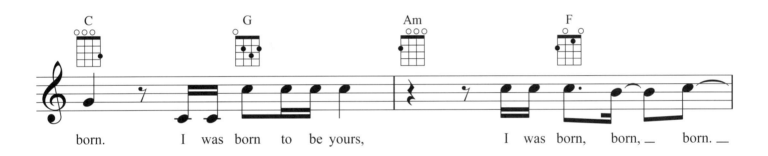

born. I was born to be yours, I was born, born, __ born. __

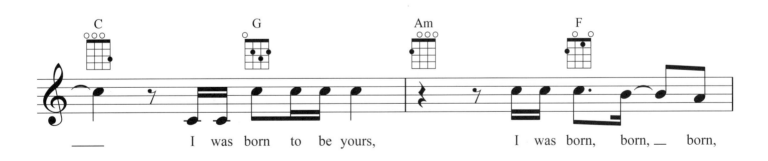

_____ I was born to be yours, I was born, born, __ born,

born. I was born to be yours, born. _____

Demons

**Words and Music by Daniel Reynolds, Benjamin McKee, Daniel Sermon,
Alexander Grant and Josh Mosser**

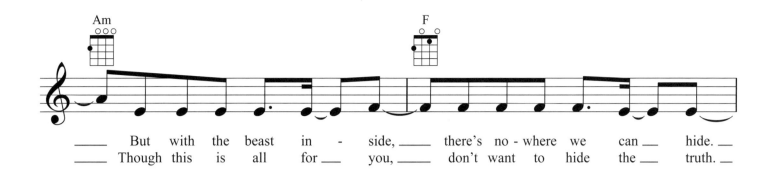

But with the beast in - side, ____ there's no - where we can ____ hide. ____
Though this is all for ____ you, ____ don't want to hide the ____ truth. ____

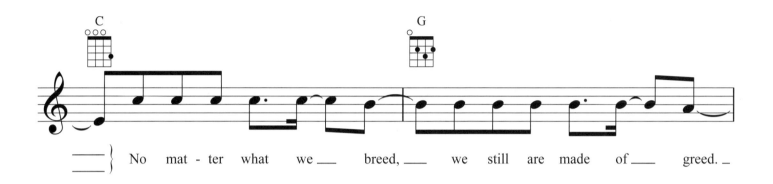

No mat - ter what we ____ breed, ____ we still are made of ____ greed. ____

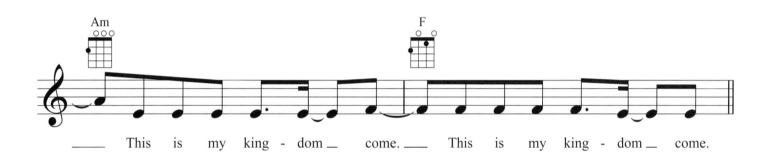

This is my king - dom ____ come. ____ This is my king - dom ____ come.

Chorus

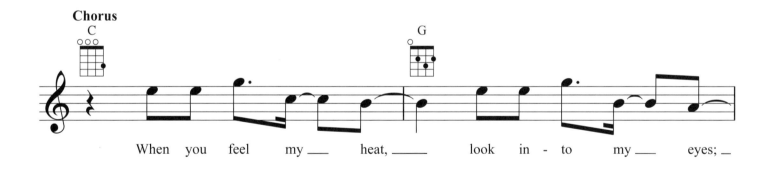

When you feel my ____ heat, ____ look in - to my ____ eyes; ____

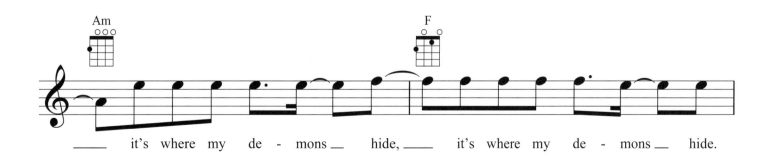

____ it's where my de - mons ____ hide, ____ it's where my de - mons ____ hide.

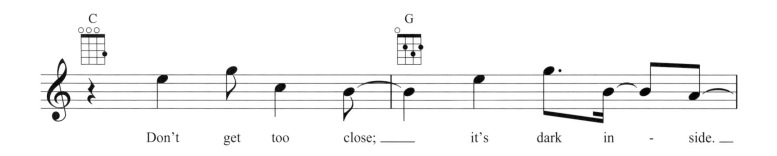

Don't   get   too   close; _____   it's   dark   in - side. __

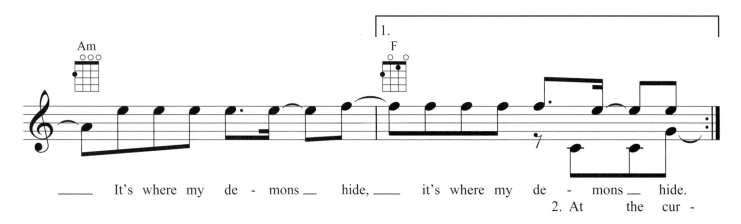

1.

_____   It's   where   my   de - mons __   hide, _____   it's   where   my   de - mons __   hide.

2. At   the   cur -

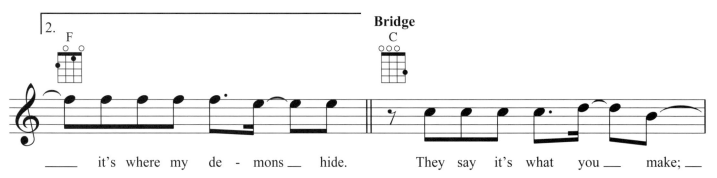

2.

Bridge

_____   it's   where   my   de - mons __   hide.   They   say   it's   what   you __   make; __

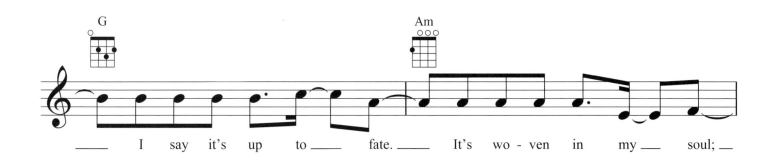

_____   I   say   it's   up   to _____   fate. _____   It's   wo - ven   in   my __   soul; __

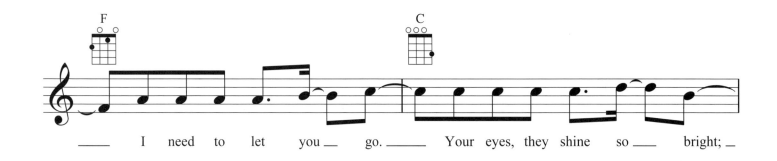

_____   I   need   to   let   you __   go. _____   Your   eyes,   they   shine   so __   bright; __

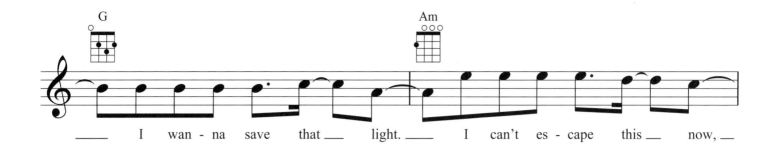

I wan - na save that ___ light. ___ I can't es - cape this ___ now, ___

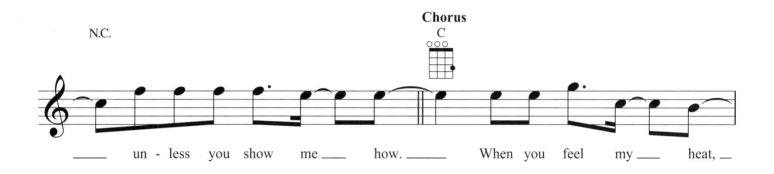

___ un - less you show me ___ how. ___ When you feel my ___ heat, ___

Chorus

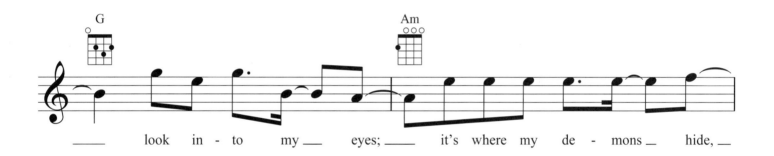

___ look in - to my ___ eyes; ___ it's where my de - mons ___ hide, ___

___ it's where my de - mons ___ hide. Don't get too close; ___ it's dark in - side. ___

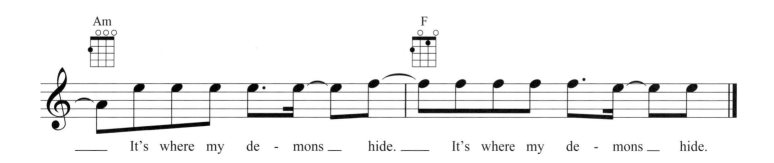

___ It's where my de - mons ___ hide. ___ It's where my de - mons ___ hide.

I Bet My Life

**Words and Music by Daniel Reynolds, Daniel Sermon,
Benjamin McKee and Daniel Platzman**

Pre-Chorus

mem-ber when _ I told _ you that's the last _____ you'll see of me? _ Re-

mem-ber when _ I broke _ you down _ to tears? _

I know I took the path _ that you would nev - er want _ for me. _

Play 1st time only

I gave you hell _ through all _____ the years. _ So

Play 2nd time only

Chorus

_____ So I, I bet my life, I bet my

life, I bet my life on you, ooh, _____ ooh. _____

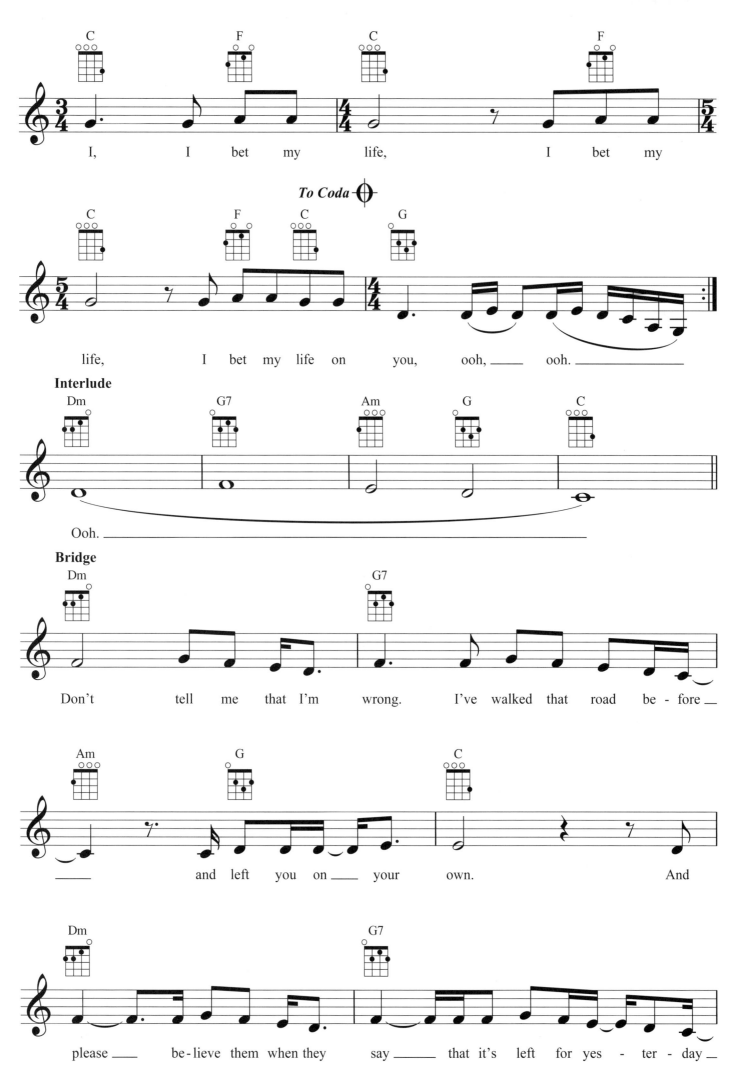

I, I bet my life, I bet my

To Coda ⊕

life, I bet my life on you, ooh, ooh.

Interlude

Ooh.

Bridge

Don't tell me that I'm wrong. I've walked that road be - fore

and left you on your own. And

please be - lieve them when they say that it's left for yes - ter - day

and the rec-ords that __ I play. __ Please for - give __

__ me for all __ I've done. So

you, ooh, __ ooh. __ I, I

bet my, I bet my, I bet my...

I, I bet my life, __ I

bet my life, __ I bet my... *(Instrumental)*

It's Time

Words and Music by Daniel Reynolds, Benjamin McKee and Daniel Sermon

I don't ev - er wan - na let you down. __

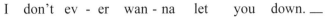

I don't ev - er wan - na leave this town. _____

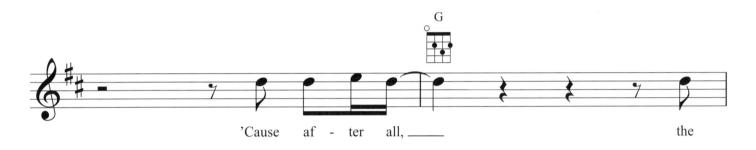

'Cause af - ter all, _____ the

Chorus

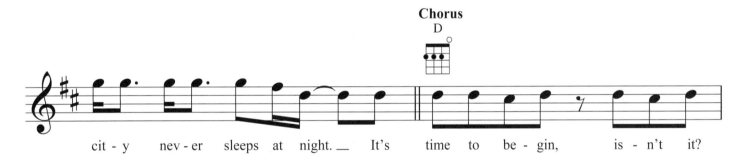

cit - y nev - er sleeps at night. __ It's time to be - gin, is - n't it?

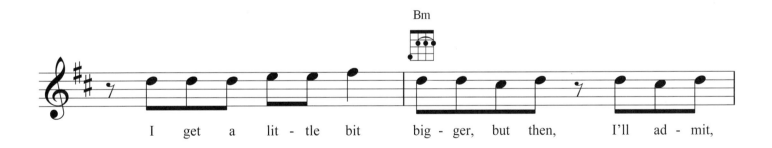

I get a lit - tle bit big - ger, but then, I'll ad - mit,

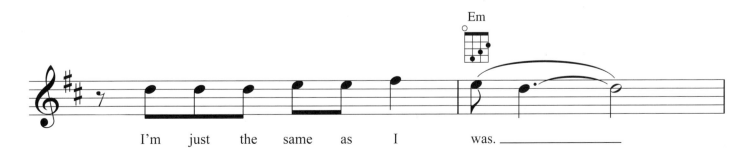

I'm just the same as I was. _____

Now, don't you un - der - stand _____ that I'm

Interlude

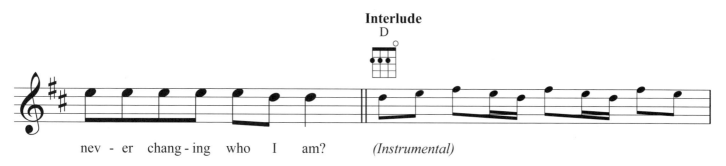

nev - er chang - ing who I am? *(Instrumental)*

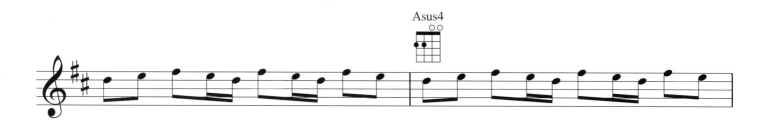

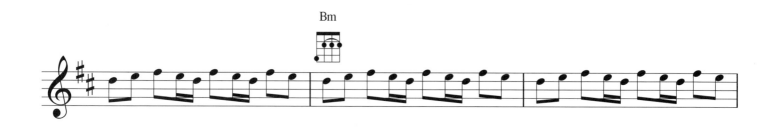

D.S. al Coda

2. So,

Chorus

Coda

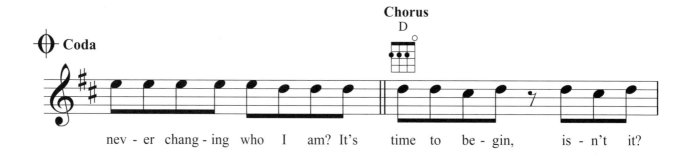

nev - er chang - ing who I am? It's time to be - gin, is - n't it?

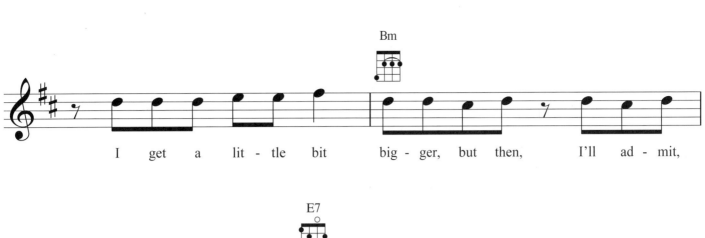

I get a lit - tle bit big - ger, but then, I'll ad - mit,

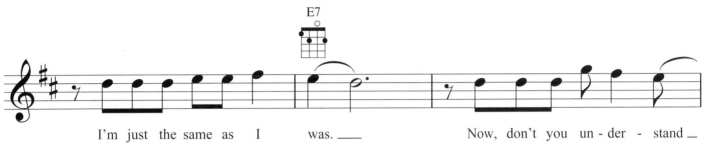

I'm just the same as I was. ___ Now, don't you un - der - stand __

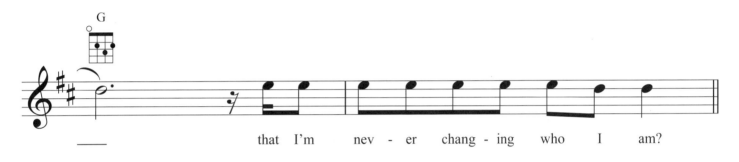

___ that I'm nev - er chang - ing who I am?

Bridge

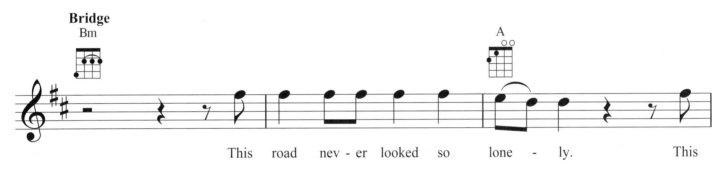

This road nev - er looked so lone - ly. This

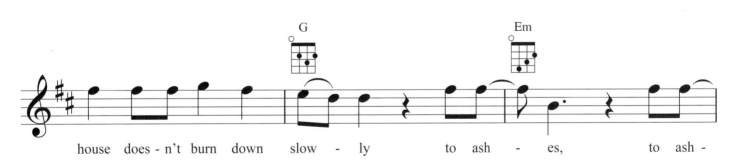

house does - n't burn down slow - ly to ash - es, to ash -

Chorus

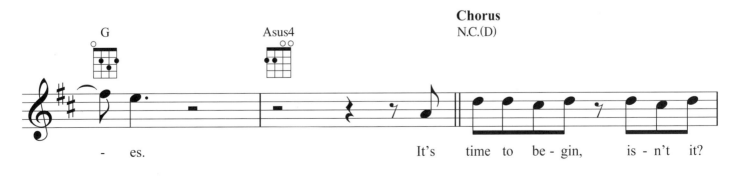

- es. It's time to be - gin, is - n't it?

(Bm)

I get a lit-tle bit big-ger, but then, I'll ad-mit, I'm just the same as I

Em   G

was. _____   Now, don't you un-der-stand ___ that I'm

Outro-Chorus

Bm

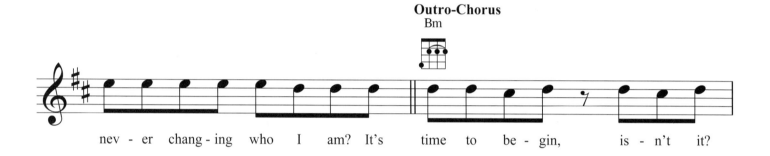

nev-er chang-ing who I am? It's time to be-gin, is-n't it?

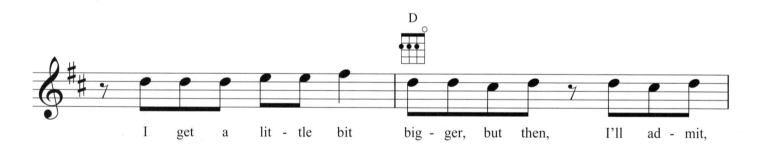

D

I get a lit-tle bit big-ger, but then, I'll ad-mit,

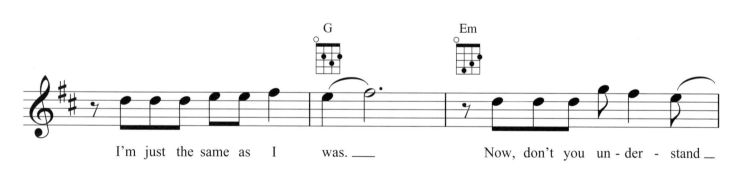

G   Em

I'm just the same as I was. ___   Now, don't you un-der-stand __

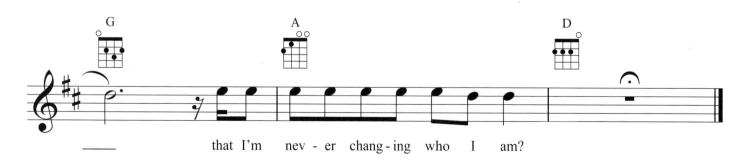

G   A   D

___ that I'm nev-er chang-ing who I am?

Next to Me

**Words and Music by Dan Reynolds, Wayne Sermon, Ben McKee,
Daniel Platzman and Alexander Grant**

First note

1. Some - thing 'bout the way that you walked in - to my liv - ing room, ___
(2.) some - thing 'bout the way that you al - ways see the pret - ty view, ___

cas - ual - ly and con - fi - dent, look - ing at the mess I am, ___ but
o - ver - look the mud and mess, al - ways look - ing ef - fort - less, ___ and

still you, still you want me.
still you, still you want me.

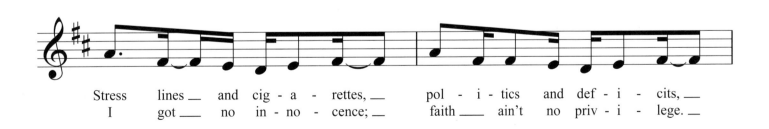

Stress lines ___ and cig - a - rettes, ___ pol - i - tics and def - i - cits, ___
I got ___ no in - no - cence; ___ faith ___ ain't no priv - i - lege. ___

late bills ___ and o - v'rag - es, scream - ing ___ and hol - ler - ing, ___ but
I am ___ a deck of cards; Vice or ___ a game of Hearts, ___ and

still you, still you want me.
still you, still you want me.

𝄋 **Chorus**

Oh, _____ I al - ways let

you down. You're shat - tered on ___ the

ground, ___ but still I find ___ you there next ___ to me.

And, oh, _____ the stu - pid things I do.

Natural

Words and Music by Dan Reynolds, Wayne Sermon, Ben McKee, Daniel Platzman, Justin Trantor, Mattias Larsson and Robin Fredricksson

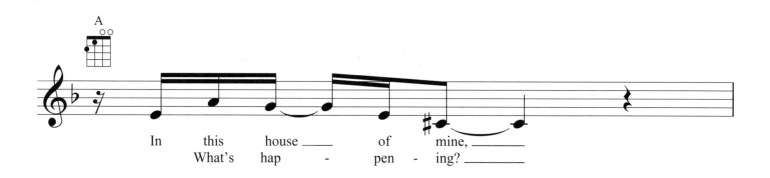

% Chorus

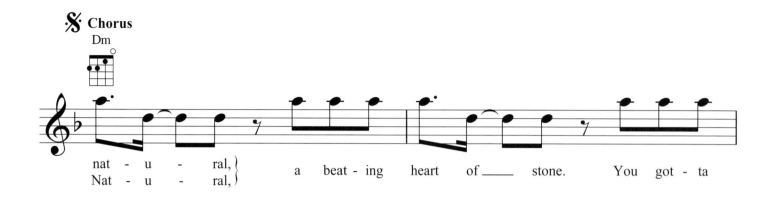

nat - u - ral,⎫
Nat - u - ral,⎭ a beat - ing heart of ____ stone. You got - ta

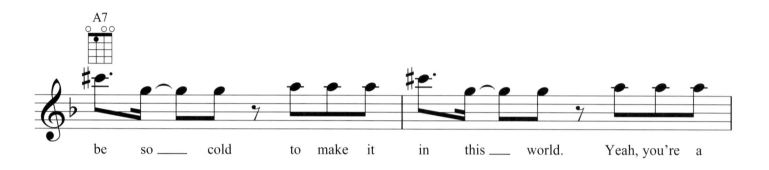

be so ____ cold to make it in this ____ world. Yeah, you're a

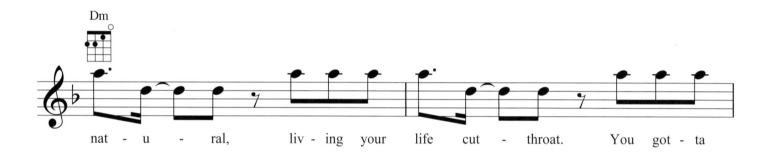

nat - u - ral, liv - ing your life cut - throat. You got - ta

Bridge

To Coda ⊕

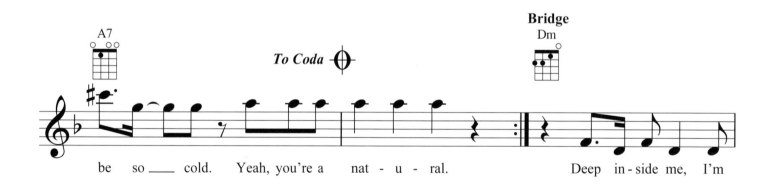

be so ____ cold. Yeah, you're a nat - u - ral. Deep in - side me, I'm

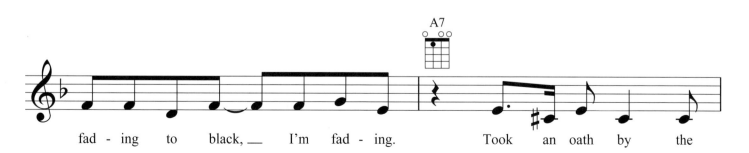

fad - ing to black, ___ I'm fad - ing. Took an oath by the

blood of my hand, ___ won't break it.   I can taste it; the

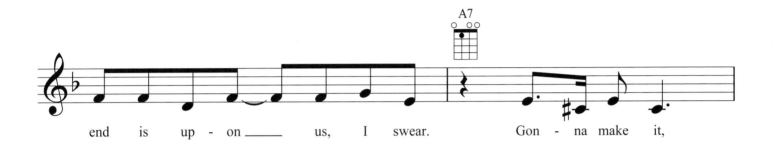

end is up - on ___ us,   I swear.   Gon - na make it,

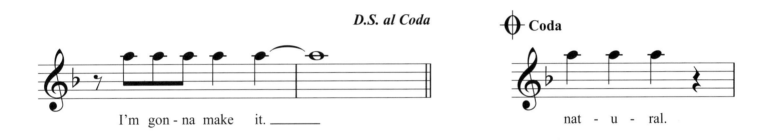

D.S. al Coda   ⊕ **Coda**

I'm gon - na make it. ___   nat - u - ral.

Outro

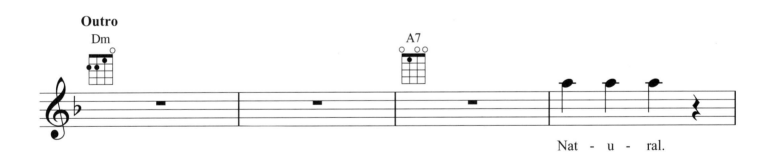

Nat - u - ral.

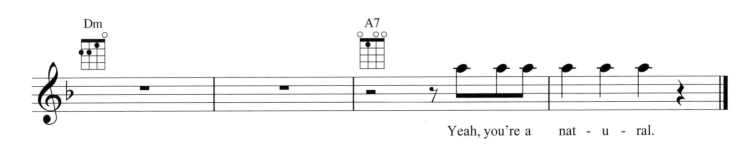

Yeah, you're a   nat - u - ral.

On Top of the World

Words and Music by Daniel Reynolds, Benjamin McKee, Daniel Sermon and Alexander Grant

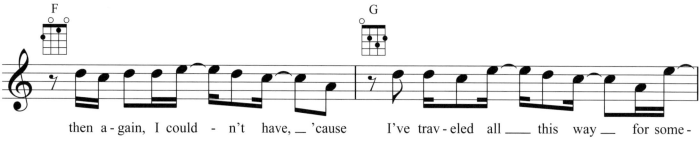

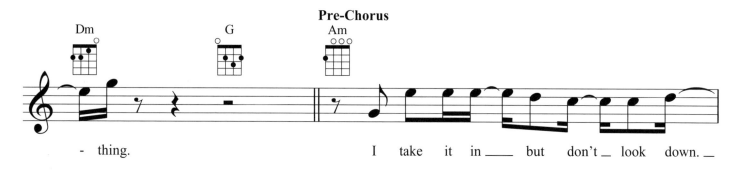

_____ can. Been dream-ing of this _____ since a child. _____ And I know _____

Bridge

_____ it's hard when you're fall - ing down, _____ and it's a

long way up when you make your round. _____ But get up _____

1.

_____ now, get up, get up _____ now. And I know _____

2. **Outro-Chorus**

_____ now. 'Cause I'm on top _____ of the world, _____ eh! I'm on top _____ of the world, _____

_____ eh! Been wait - ing on this _____ for a while _____

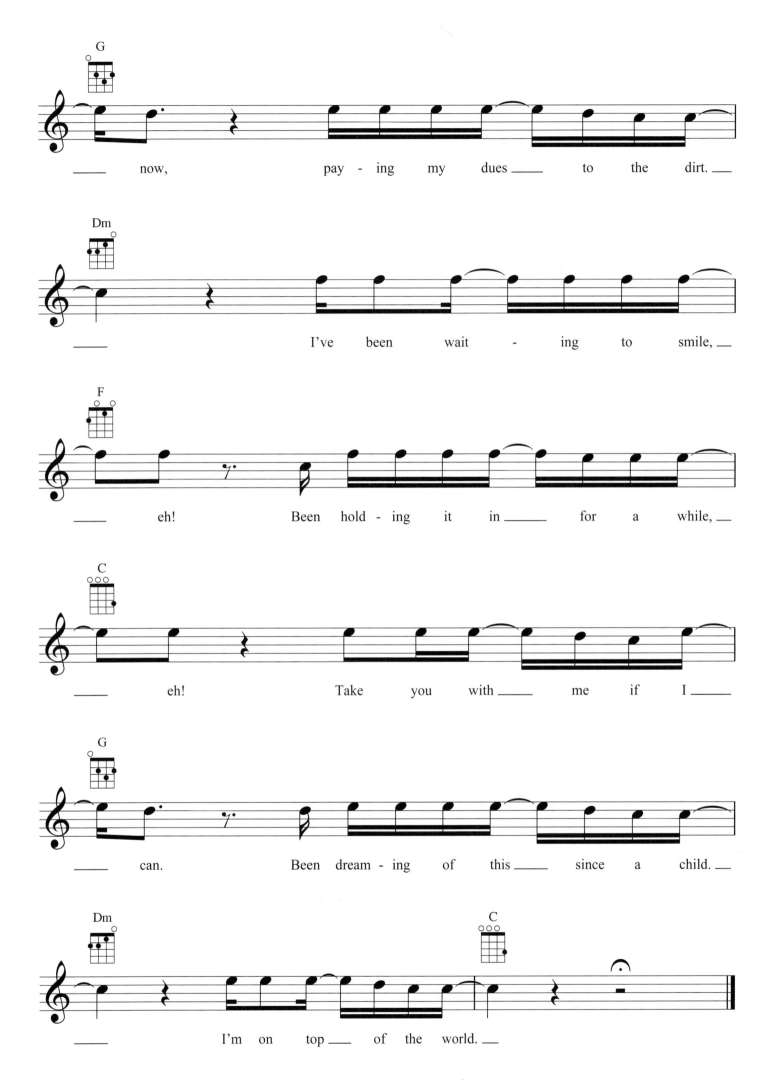

____ now, pay - ing my dues ____ to the dirt. ____

____ I've been wait - ing to smile, ____

____ eh! Been hold - ing it in ____ for a while, ____

____ eh! Take you with ____ me if I ____

____ can. Been dream - ing of this ____ since a child. ____

____ I'm on top ____ of the world. ____

Thunder

Words and Music by Dan Reynolds, Wayne Sermon, Ben McKee,
Daniel Platzman, Alexander Grant and Jayson DeZuzio

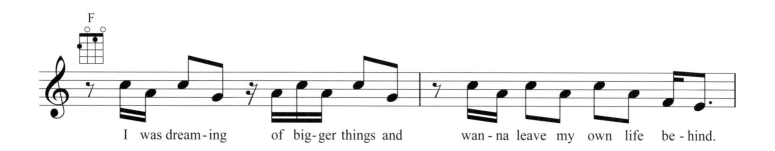

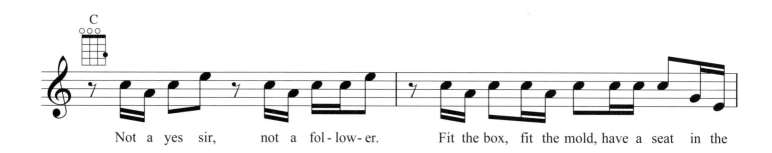

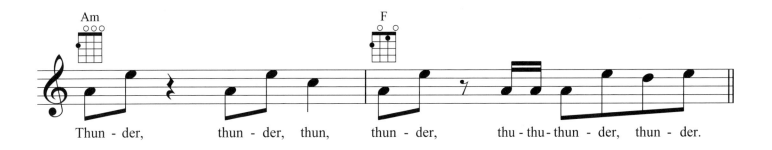

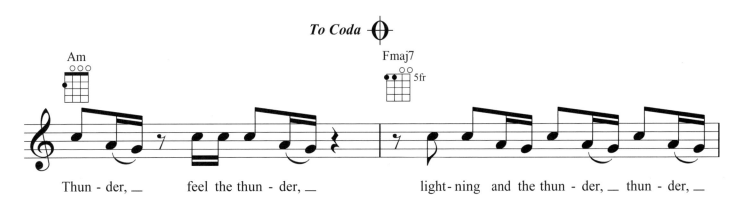

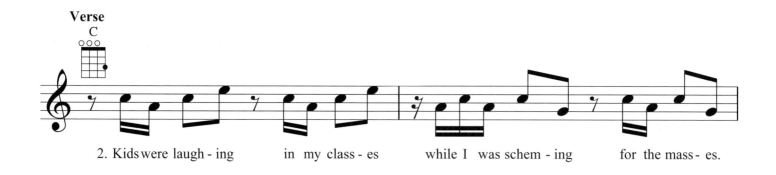

Verse

2. Kids were laugh-ing   in my class-es   while I was schem-ing   for the mass-es.

"Who do you think __ you are ____   dream-ing 'bout be-ing a big ___ star?" ____

You say you're bas-ic,   you say you're eas-y,   you're al-ways rid-ing   in the back seat.

D.S. al Coda

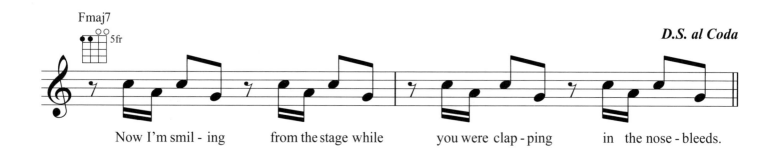

Now I'm smil-ing   from the stage while   you were clap-ping   in the nose-bleeds.

Coda

light-ning   and   the   thun-der, ___   thun-der. ___

Interlude

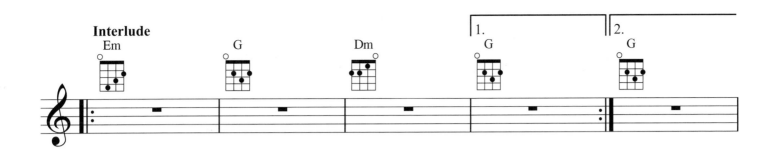

Thun - der, __ feel the thun - der, __ light - ning and the thun - der, __ thun - der. __

Chorus

Thun - der, __ feel the thun - der, __ light - ning and the thun - der, __ thun - der. __

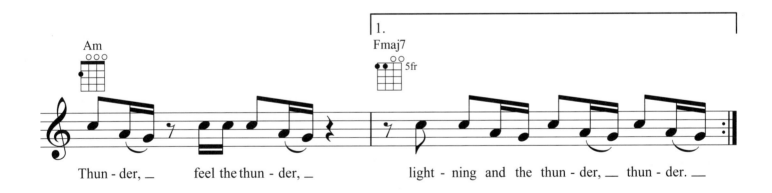

Thun - der, __ feel the thun - der, __ light - ning and the thun - der, __ thun - der. __

light - ning and the thun - der, __ thun - der. __

Walking the Wire

Words and Music by Dan Reynolds, Wayne Sermon, Ben McKee, Daniel Platzman,
Justin Trantor, Mattias Larsson and Robin Fredricksson

fraid of fall - ing, then don't look down.　(Ooh.) _____ But we
tears we'll cry, __ but those tears will fade.　(Ooh.) _____ It's the

took the step __ and we took the leap; __　and we'll
price we pay __ when it comes to love; __　and we'll

take what __ comes, __　take what __ comes. __ } Feel the wind __
take what __ comes, __　take what __ comes. __

Pre-Chorus

_____ in your hair, __　feel the rush _____ way up here. __

𝄋 **Chorus**

__ We're walk - ing the wi - re,　love. __　We're walk - ing the wi -

-re,   love. ___   We're gon - na be high - er   up. ___

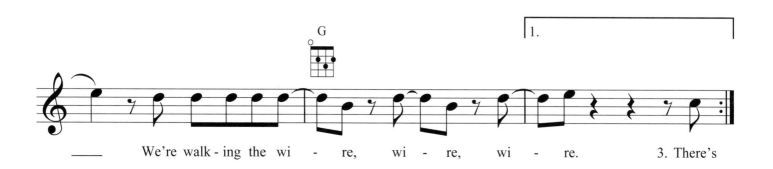

1.

___ We're walk - ing the wi - re,   wi - re,   wi - re.   3. There's

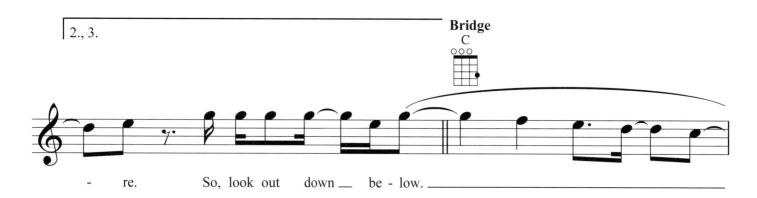

2., 3.   **Bridge**

-re.   So, look out down ___ be - low. ___

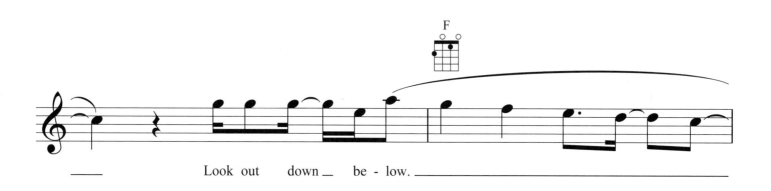

___   Look out down ___ be - low. ___

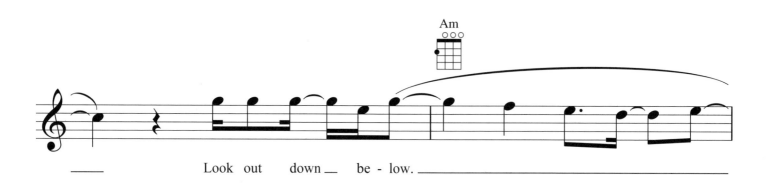

___   Look out down ___ be - low. ___

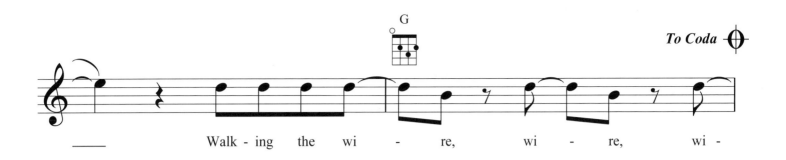

Walk - ing the wi - re, wi - re, wi -

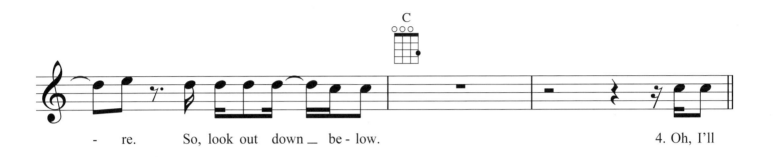

- re. So, look out down _ be - low. 4. Oh, I'll

Verse

take your hand _ when thun - der roars; _ and I'll

hold you close, _ I'll stay the course. _ I

prom - ise you _ from up a - bove _ that we'll take what _ comes, _

take what __ comes, __ love. __ We're walk - ing the wi -

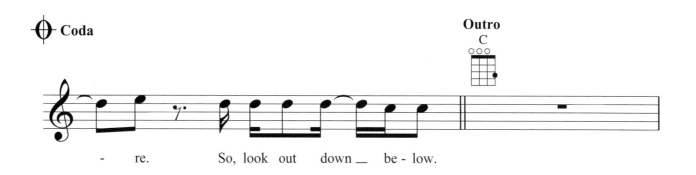

Coda **Outro**

\- re. So, look out down __ be - low.

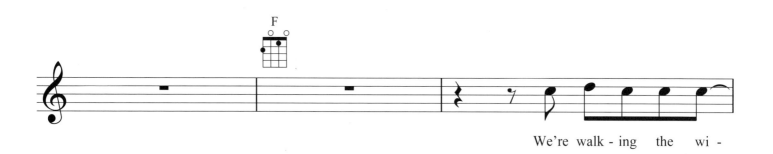

We're walk - ing the wi -

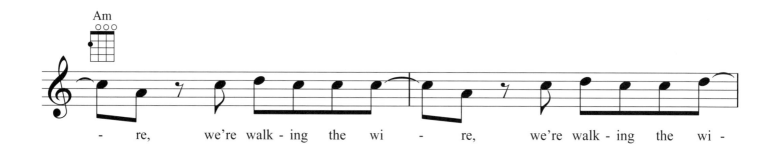

\- re, we're walk - ing the wi - re, we're walk - ing the wi -

\- re, wi - re, wi - re.

Radioactive

Words and Music by Daniel Reynolds, Benjamin McKee, Daniel Sermon,
Alexander Grant and Josh Mosser

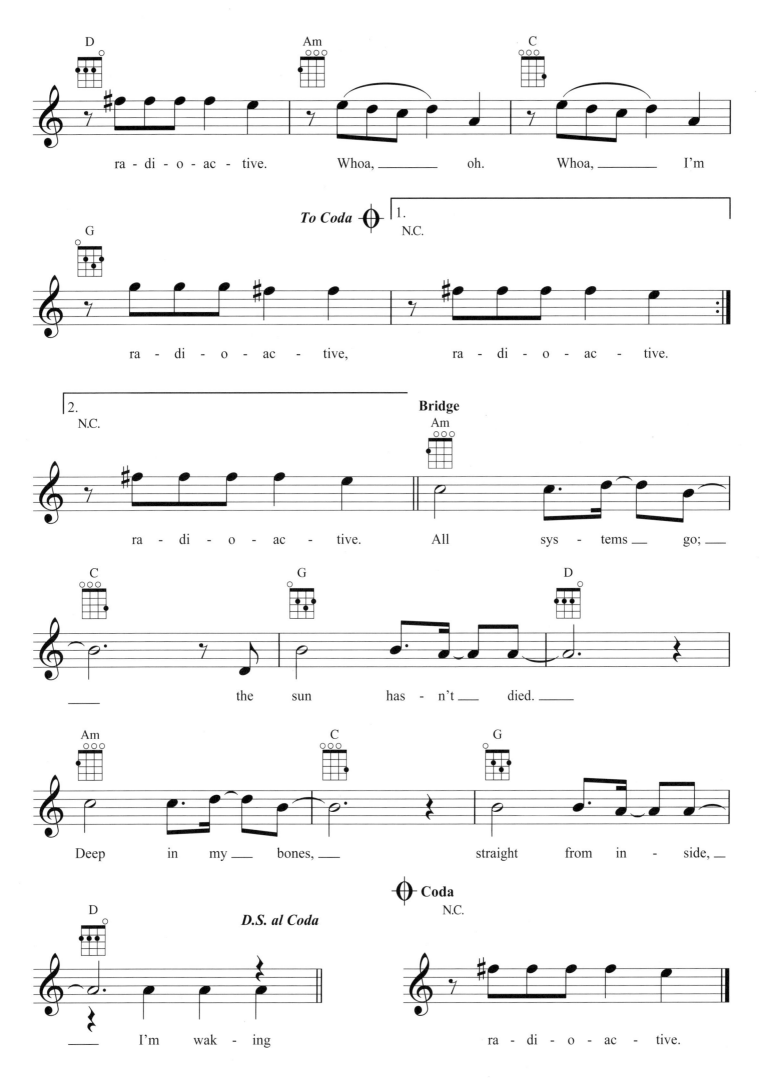

Warriors

**Words and Music by Alexander Grant, Daniel Reynolds, Daniel Sermon,
Benjamin McKee, Daniel Platzman and Joshua Mosser**

Whatever It Takes

Words and Music by Dan Reynolds, Wayne Sermon, Ben McKee,
Daniel Platzman and Joel Little

First note

Verse
Moderately

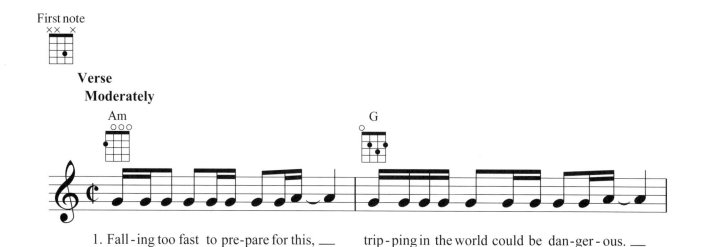

1. Fall-ing too fast to pre-pare for this, __ trip-ping in the world could be dan-ger-ous. __

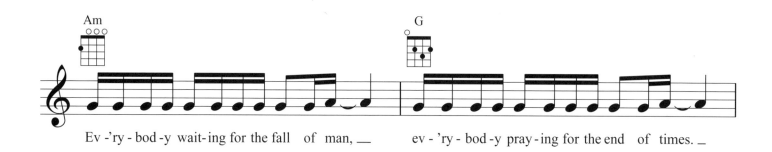

Ev-'ry-bod-y cir-cl-ing, it's vul-tur-ous, __ neg-a-tive, __ nep-o-tist. __

Ev-'ry-bod-y wait-ing for the fall of man, __ ev-'ry-bod-y pray-ing for the end of times. __

Ev-'ry-bod-y hop-ing they could be the one. __ I was born to run, __ I was born for this.

Pre-Chorus

Whip, whip, run me like a race horse. Pull me like a rip - cord, break me down and build me up. I want to be the slip, slip word up - on your lip, lip. Let - ter that you rip, rip. Break me down and build me up, what - ev - er it takes, ___

Chorus

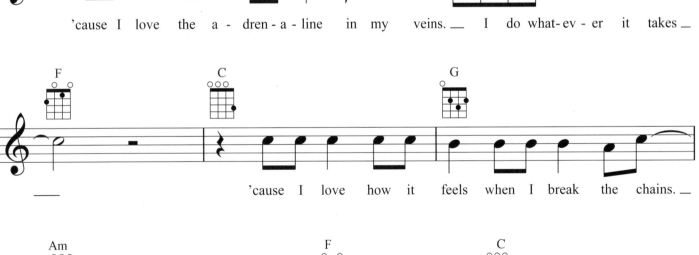

'cause I love the a - dren - a - line in my veins. ___ I do what-ev - er it takes ___ ___ 'cause I love how it feels when I break the chains. ___ ___ What - ev - er it takes, ___ you

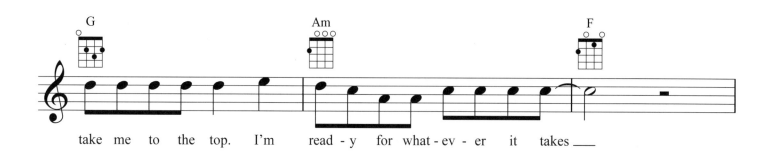

take me to the top. I'm read-y for what-ev-er it takes ___

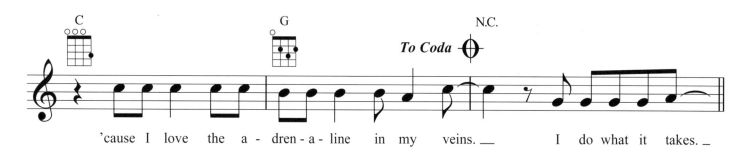

'cause I love the a-dren-a-line in my veins. ___ I do what it takes. _

Verse

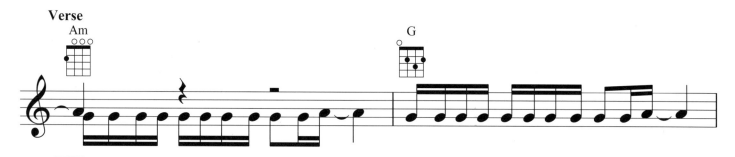

2. Al-ways had a fear of be-ing typ-i-cal, ___ look-ing at my bod-y, feel-ing mis-'ra-ble. ___

Al-ways hang-ing on-to the vi-su-al, ___ I want to be ___ in-vis-i-ble. ___

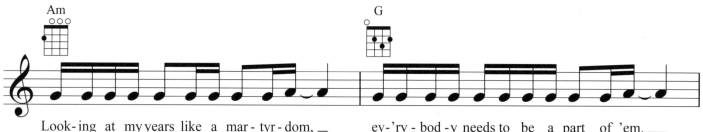

Look-ing at my years like a mar-tyr-dom, _ ev-'ry-bod-y needs to be a part of 'em. ___

Nev-er be e-nough, I'm the prod-i-gal son. ___ I was born to run, ___ I was born for this.

Coda

Bridge

I do what it takes. Hyp-o-crit-i-cal, e-go-tis-ti-cal, don't want to be the

par-en-thet-i-cal, hy-po-thet-i-cal. Work-ing on-to some-thing that I'm proud of,

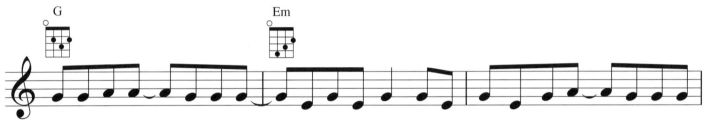

out of the box, __ an e-pox - y to the world and the vi - sion we've lost. __ I'm an a -

pos-tro-phe, I'm just a sym-bol to re-mind you that there's more to see. I'm just a

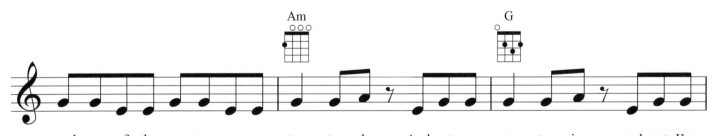

prod-uct of the sys-tem, a ca-tas-tro-phe. And yet a mas-ter-piece and yet I'm

half dis-eased. And when I am de-ceased, at least I go down to the grave and die

hap - pi - ly.   Leave the bod - y of my soul to be a   part   of me.

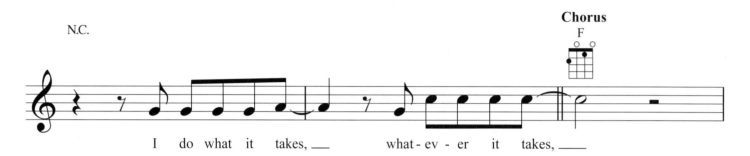

I   do what it   takes, ___   what - ev - er   it   takes, ___

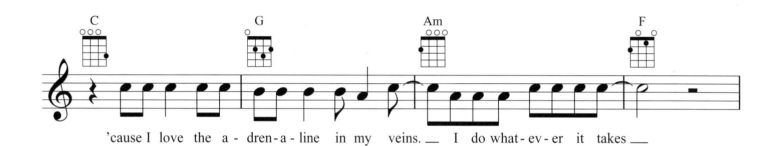

'cause I love the a - dren - a - line in my veins. ___   I do what - ev - er it takes ___

'cause I love how it   feels when I break the chains. _   What - ev - er it   takes, ___

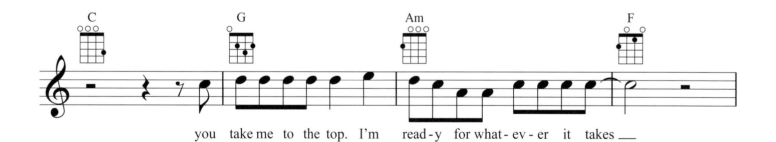

you   take me to the top. I'm   read - y for what - ev - er it takes ___

'cause I love the a - dren - a - line in my veins. ___   I do what it takes. ___